Strategies to push through

Comfort zone to Creative zone

Deuteronomy 31:6

6 Be strong and courageous. Do not be afraid or

terrified because of them, for the LORD your God

goes with you; he will never leave you nor forsake

you."

John 14:27

27 Peace I leave with you; my peace I give you. I do

not give to you as the world gives. Do not let your

hearts be troubled and do not be afraid

2 Timothy 1:7

7 For the Spirit God gave us does not make us timid, but gives us power, love and self-discipline.

Joshua 1:9

9 Have I not commanded you? Be strong and courageous. Do not be afraid; do not be discouraged, for the LORD your God will be with you wherever you go."

Isaiah 54:4

4 "Do not be afraid; you will not be put to shame. Do not fear disgrace; you will not be humiliated.

KICK

Doubt,

Fear

Insecurity

Procrastination

Hesitation

INTRODUCTION

INTRODUCTION

The beautiful gift of a new life comes with the ugly end of another life. It seems the creation of the human race has been divinely set that way. A beginning must have an end, the cycle of life. This knowledge, we would assume would keep us prepared. Unfortunately, this knowledge is not enough to stop the feeling and pain associated with loss. No one is spared, we will all have our time with death. We will witness and experience our share of loss and pain. How we cope and move forward during a loss will determine the quality of our years left. If someone offers you a shoulder to lean on during your difficult time, lean on them. It is not easy to be a pillar for another. That shoulder that you are leaning on, might also be carrying a burden. Their burden might not be visible to you but always consider the real possibility that they might harbor personal struggles.

It was the summer of 2014 when she left me, then came the fall of 2015 and he left me as well. I lost both my parents within two years. It is said that with the emergence of life, there is the certainty of death_____ a sad reality we never want to face. While I was no stranger to loss due to the death of my son in 2007, It was still inconceivable to think I'd become an orphan in such a short time. Nevertheless, life goes on. I make an effort to support and assist family and friends when I am able to do so comfortably. For so long I had heard the popular saying, "you cannot pour out of an empty tank, fuel yourself first", but I never truly absorbed the meaning till now. You and only you are responsible for your peace. You need to look in the mirror and speak peace, love, care and happiness to yourself. This has gotten me through these rough and painful years. Yet, I hear friends going through their storms saying, "Friends have let me down", "I have learned not to depend on anyone", "Life has taught me that I am on my own". No matter the words used, the basic premise is ____they have learned to be their own source of comfort.

There is already so much burden in our hearts why intentionally add to it? It took a while but I have learned to let guilt roll off my back. I do not feel any sense of guilt for not being able to support others as I would like. I do my best now and move forward. Carrying guilt is an additional burden that I cannot afford to keep. Prior to going through my storm, I worried about what others "thought" about me. There was a sense of "obligation to please" others. But life experiences have shown me that people will not treat you as well as you treat them. I have learned that, this is OK. They are struggling with their own issues. My mother always said, "When a blind man leads another blind man or a group of seeing men, they will all fall in a ditch", moral ____ if you choose to be reckless, then you will suffer the same faith as those who are clueless. Some people are smart but they prefer to follow the "crowd". Walking like a sheep to the slaughter house. There is absolutely no need to "follow the crowd". Societal demands make it hard but it is possible to stand out and be yourself. The result of trusting other people's instincts and ignoring yours often leads to failure.

Most entrepreneurs I have spoken with have similar complaints, especially when their business is new. Many are surprised that the support they expected from friends and family is almost non-existent. Depending on your friends and family to support and grow your business or help with your problems is presumptuous.

Do you have any idea what they are going through?

Have you paused to think or ask about their well -being genuinely?

We get busy in our lives, trying to quickly fix any problems we have. It is hard wired in the human brain to survive and thrive. The problem is that we are selfish and seek to fully experience all that life has to offer however, we must engage in the uncomfortable tasks. Some, we have control over and many we cannot control, such as death. It is difficult to move from our comfort zone but think about the motivation a dying person possesses. Imagine a person who was informed that they have only two months left to live, if they have a bucket list, they will try to get all the items on their list done. The reality that time is truly limited sets in. There will be things they will rush to do. They will no longer allow fear to cripple them.

Imagine that!

Isn't it amazing how we waste so much time when we assume we have abundant time? We give fear a lot of our precious time. It is amazing what we can achieve when our time is limited and we push fear aside. We toss caution to the wind without a care in the world. When the fear of the unknown is known, what else will there be to stop us from attaining our aspirations? That point where we act without restriction, is the point our lives sprout.

Chapter One

Bracing Moments

"It has been impossible to get contracts, I have tried for over two weeks now" as the words came out of my mouth my heart sank. Here I was, learning, reading, listening and teaching about the power of the tongue and positive thinking, and I was doing the exact opposite. She listened intently and reminded me in a highly optimistic tone about the power of the tongue, my views and practice of positive thinking, and I realized I had briefly lost my faith .She had the strong sense that nothing is impossible and something wonderful is about to happen. She encouraged me to stay positive and proactive. Inadvertently, I was using my words to create a self-fulfilling prophecy and not a prophecy that I wanted to materialize.   At this point, I realized the need for refreshers. Knowing is not enough, we need refreshers, reminders and maintenance of our state of awareness. This is why we read, take a bath/shower, pray daily and exercise. Good habits are hard and require daily maintenance. Failure to maintain what we have learned will adversely affect our actions.

Proverbs 18:21 " Death and life are in the power of the tongue: and they that love it shall eat the fruit thereof." The tongue has no bones but commands the most powerful state. The words you speak hold the power to destroy or build. Power to create new expectations and win or lose. Power to build relationships or to destroy them. Power to uplift people or to pull them down.Most times we don't understand the impact of our words on both ourselves and others, until it is too late. True knowledge of the power of our words will make us more encouraging and less discouraging. You would also hear a lot less of "It's impossible ......," "I can not..." or "It can't be done ....etc. "—all idiomatic expression which sabotage our talents, power and limit our future.

The words we speak into existence in our lives create the reality we live out. Unfortunately, Success is a scary notion and we often get a negative reality because we subconsciously sabotage our success simply by using language that undermine our opinions, magnifies our problems and takes away our confidence to handle them. Whatsoever path your words lead, your mind, body and heart will unavoidably follow.

When you use positive communication about yourself and your ability to learn new skills, achieve your goals and handle pressure, then that's what tends to show up externally. Likewise, if you're always saying things that affirm incompetence, reverberate despair, nurture anxiety then that will also shape your experience. In time your reality will morph to mirror your words. Hence, it's exceedingly essential to be thoughtful about the words you use and deliberate about speaking in ways that empower and expand rather than degrade and disparage.

Unfortunately, most people in general underestimate the power they possess to effect positive change. This is reverberated in the words they use to describe themselves and their circumstances. By Engaging in actions that paint them as helpless victims of forces beyond their control, devoid of the power and influence to modify their situation, they render themselves just that. It is a vicious cycle as they gather more manifestation to confirm their impotence.

A subtle difference in our attitude and thinking can make a major difference in our future. It can be as simple as the our daily language. It's the difference in how you talk to yourself or others. Its making a conscious effort to quit saying what you don't want and to start saying and focusing on what you do want. It's faith—believing in the best and moving toward the best even when you do not see it.

As seen in Matthew 17:20, "He replied, "Because you have so little faith. Truly I tell you, if you have faith as small as a mustard seed, you can say to this mountain, 'Move from here to there,' and it will move. Nothing will be impossible for you."

Replace the negative with a positive thought , for instance "What if somebody doesn't respond?" versus "What if they do respond?" or "What if someone says no?" versus "What if they say yes?" or "What if it doesn't work out?" versus, "What if it does work out?" Apply the positive questioning.

When you start thinking and saying what you really want, then your mind is mechanically altered and pulls you in that positive direction. And sometimes it is that easy—

just a little maneuver in vocabulary that illustrates your mental attitude and belief. Our language can also affect how others perform and behave around us. Our value are sometimes just a matter of language. But here is the great news. You can start this process anytime. We each have individual power we can tap into. Tapping into that ability requires self-awareness of where you are and where you need to get to.

Chapter Two

Comfortable and

Complacent

Comfort zone, yes! The Merriam Webster dictionary defines comfort as a "state or situation in which you are relaxed and do not have any physically unpleasant feelings caused by pain, heat, cold, etc.: a state or feeling of being less worried, upset, frightened, etc., during a time of trouble or emotional pain." It is no wonder, humans love to get in and stay in comfortable situations or as popularly called "comfort zone". Who likes to be inconvenienced? It is being used widespread these days that many people think "comfort zone" is some vestige of ancient motivational psychological term. Some even think it is a "cheesy" corporate motivational tag line.

The fact is that a "comfort zone" is a useful concept that can enlighten us to our situations. It reveals our unwillingness to embrace risk and make difficult transformations that can lead to our personal growth. Being comfortable often translates to stunted growth and complacency. *The comfort zone, as defined by Lifehacker, is a "behavioral space where your activities and behaviors fit a routine and pattern that minimizes stress and risk" — the operative words here being stress and risk.* Leaving our comfort zone can lead to stress. Stress is a disparaging word. We hear stress and we are immediately uncomfortable. This is for good reason because stress causes unappealing side effects. Weight gain, high blood pressure, anxiety, etc. a plethora of side effects are associated with stress. Stress, however, when handled sensibly can lead to growth- personal and professional growth. If a situation is uncomfortable, it will either force us to endure pain or serve as a catalyst for us to sprout.

We love our comfort. Stress forces us to act. Sometimes it is the exact push needed. When we are within out comfort zone, all our elements are relaxed. We are in a familiar place. Imagine taking antibiotics for an ailment and suddenly after some months of use, the antibiotic is no longer effective. This is because the antibiotic has gotten used to the environment. The drug becomes resistant and is no longer an effective treatment option. Alternatively, imagine a person who has worked for 10years at the same job and does not move to another organization. That person has stunted their growth. For instance, Joe, is an accountant, Joe who started working right after graduation from school with DoTouch Company. Joe becomes certified with his CPA, CFM and DCFM etc. while at this company but he is still working as an accountant. He has not grown much, maybe a 2% raise or a reimbursement for his certifications is the most he has gotten. If Joe moves, he can earn at least 40% more than his current salary. Joe is not willing to move because he is comfortable. He is used to his daily routine and tasks. He can close his eyes and do his job. Not much has changed in his duties. He has become very familiar with the company and its processes.

Karen, a former coworker informs him that she now works with KayPez Consulting and they are paying her almost 50% more than she earned while with DoTouch Company. She encourages Joe to make the move. Karen is a risk taker and comfortable with shaking her zone. Joe is more risk adverse and does not like to "rock the boat", so to speak.

Joe needs a little push to be able to move out of his comfort zone. If there were to be a re-organization going on, where employees were laid off, Joe might reconsider. He would be naturally stressed and eager to act. Joe is comfortable and feels "at home" in his current company. Joe is used to the consistent and predictable work flow at his current position.

Pause and think: Would you be willing to step on hot coal?

If you were told stepping on hot coal will get you a million dollars, now, would you step on hot coal? It is always difficult to move out of our comfort zone but if we knew the reward, we might act differently. As creatures of comfort, WE embrace comfort. We like predictability- to know what is next. We do not like the unknown. This is part of the reason, change is so difficult for us.

Chapter Three

YO(U)R STORY

In your story, you (u) matter the most! Always remember that. Somehow it always seems that the aspirations we desire most is on the other side of a "mountain". How we get over or around that mountain becomes the focus. If we can't jump over it, then certainly we should hop like a rabbit or move like a cheetah, gazelle or a lion. The point is we move. Move until we figure out how to get over that "mountain".

You are the only person who can change your current situation. Everyone suffers from self-doubt. Making decisions based on the "feelings" will rob us of our success. No one "feels" like doing the demanding things in life. There is a five second window to make good decision and resist hesitation. Mel Robins in her book, the 5 second rule, wrote that, "Hesitation is the kiss of death. You might hesitate for a just nanosecond, but that's all it takes. That one small hesitation triggers a mental system that's designed to stop you. And it happens in less than—you guessed it—five seconds."

Small, easy decisions compound to matter. Everything "bleeds" into the other. Everything we do is interconnected. There is a ripple effect in the daily routine and activities we do. Recognize that tragedies will occur in our life. We need the fortitude to endure. The ability to keep going when times are hard. The ability to learn new skills, endure and do what must be done! When we ask what we need to do? We might not like the answer. When we change our mindset and ask, what can we do that we enjoy? Then we can push ourselves to do it daily consistently and with conviction.

What is success to you?

What does success look like, paint a picture?

What is your purpose?

What is your passion?

If you know your purpose are passionate about it, do you have the skills to move forward with it?

Are you willing to work at perfecting your skills for your passion?

Your accomplishments will be a result of your focus and skills. It is not enough to have passion. It is not enough to want to succeed, we must push past our fear to succeed. We hesitate and kill our dreams. Below are some experiences on moving past self-doubt and fear by some successful entrepreneurs. Do not compare yourself, create yourself. Creativity is the key to attaining our success.

Are you paralyzed with fear? That's a good sign. Fear is good. Like self-doubt, fear is an indicator. Fear tells us what we must do. Remember our rule of thumb: The more scared we are of a work or calling, the more certain we can be that we have to do it.

Resistance is experienced as fear; the degree of fear equates the strength of Resistance. Therefore, the more fear we feel about a specific enterprise, the more certain we can be that that enterprise is important to us and to the growth of our soul."

–Steven Pressfield, *The War of Art*

"What we need to do is say, "What's the smallest, tiniest thing that I can master and what's the scariest thing I can do in front of the smallest number of people that can teach me how to dance with the fear?" Once we get good at that, we just realize that it's not fatal. And it's not intellectually realize – we've lived something that wasn't fatal. And that idea is what's so key — because then you can do it a little bit more."

–Seth Godin

"When you are thinking about doing something and it feels scary, when it feels like this big lion is waiting at the finish line and he's roaring and he's ferocious and he's going to *tear you apart... you should just run toward that lion anyway. Run to the roar."*

–Tina Essmaker

"It's a terrible thing, I think, in life to wait until you're ready. I have this feeling now that actually no one is ever ready to do anything. There's almost no such thing as ready. There's only now. And you may as well do it now. I mean, I say that confidently as if I'm about to go bungee jumping or something — I'm not. I'm not a crazed risk taker. But I do think that, generally speaking, now is as good a time as any."

–Hugh Laurie

"I was in my late twenties, so I had a business, but nobody knew who I was at the time. I was headed to the Virgin Islands and I had a very pretty girl waiting for me, so I was, umm, determined to get there on time.

At the airport, my final flight to the Virgin Islands was canceled because of maintenance or something. It was the last flight out that night. I thought this was ridiculous, so I went and chartered a private airplane to take me to the

Virgin Islands, which I did not have the money to do. Then,
I picked up a small blackboard, wrote "Virgin Airlines.
$29." on it, and went over to the group of people who had
been on the flight that was canceled. I sold tickets for the
rest of the seats on the plane, used their money to pay for
the chartered plane, and we all went to the Virgin Islands
that night."

—Richard Branson

FACING F.E.A.R. Mindset

"F-E-A-R has two meanings: 'Forget Everything and Run' or 'Face Everything and Rise.' The choice is yours." — *Zig Ziglar*

"What the mind can conceive and believe, and the heart desire, you can achieve." — *Norman Vincent Peale*

Consciously and subconsciously we attract negative issues to us. If you are always thinking about the negative aspects in life, misery will always keep your thoughts company. As the saying goes, "misery loves company", kick misery out of your thoughts.

We need to control and direct our thoughts to better and more appealing things. No matter how terrible or problematic a situation seems, our constant negative thoughts about it, makes it twice as problematic.

So how do we control our thought exactly? We can start be appreciating everything good in our lives. Stop complaining and reaffirming the negative aspects in our lives. A fear based mindset will allow problems increase. It is the universal law of attraction at work or something more spiritual.

Ever noticed, when you say, you will not get something, you really don't?

Speak positive results on your situation, this is how you gain control of your thoughts. Refrain from complaining and worrying instead bless the day and speak blessings on your situation. Talk back to the inside voice with the "cant's". The voice in our heads set out to "protect" us from disappointments. They are a defense mechanism due to prior experiences or fear. Think about it, successful people do not gossip. In fact they do not spend time talking about others either as a boost or not. Imagine that employee, you always thought, they will get promoted. They also, might be expecting a promotion. You have just added to their positive energy and will, knowingly or not. You could have focused that thought on you getting promoted. There are many ways we give out our power without even realizing it, just by engaging in unproductive acts.

There are many biblical verses that can help. Remember that in Joshua 1:9, Christ says (9) Have I not commanded you? Be strong and courageous. Do not be afraid; do not be discouraged, for the LORD your God will be with you wherever you go." And Matthew 6:34, (34) Therefore do not worry about tomorrow, for tomorrow will worry about itself. Each day has enough trouble of its own.

This will end the same!

Not again

Why is this happening to me?

Why can't I ever get a break?

I will never be able to handle this.

What's the use? No one cares anyway.

Unfortunately, we get so engrossed in our daily routine that we do not even realize that inside voice giving us the negative thought. Becoming more self-aware is the first step to getting rid of that voice. When you are aware, you will know immediately when your thoughts turn negative. You will make conscious efforts to redirect your thoughts to something positive and uplifting. You realize the dismal reality that you were about to create for yourself, just by that singular thought.

You have the power to change your thinking. You have the ability to control your results. This can be accomplished by staying on the offensive and counterattacking with enabling thoughts and words that instill confidence, courage and determination. When the negative thought appears, recognize it and put it down. Verbalize if needed. Some are able to internally talk down a situation and think positively and others might have to speak it out. Alternatively, you can write it out and then read it out!

Think about a time when you got so upset at your spouse and drafted a page or more long email but never hit the "send" button. Or a situation where you were so upset at work and you walked outside and yelled on top of your lungs. Treat this the same way. Like you need to get air, go drive, walk, write but get that negative thought out.

Take fear down with these scripture words;

Norman Peale said "Believe in yourself! Have faith in your abilities! Without a humble and reasonable confidence in your own powers you cannot be successful or happy." Some scriptures verses, such as Isaiah 43:5, says "Do not be afraid, for I am with you; I will bring your children from the east and gather you from the west. Believe the great fact that God is with you. And with God's help, what can stand in your way? If you are a believer and a christian then, I have no doubt that you believe in God or a Supreme being. To truly believe that God is with you, on your side, by your side, in you, helping you, requires strong faith. When you have this overwhelming faith in God, when you really believe in Him, and then call upon Him, He will answer and show you mighty things that you never knew. As you practice this thought, you will become aware that He is also showing you a greater truth. "Do not be afraid, for I am with you" (Isaiah 43:5) is probably one of the greatest statements ever made in the history of human life on this earth. We are taught this but we do not keep it in mind. Think big. And think the biggest thought of all—that you are not alone, that God will always help you."

1 Peter 5:6-7; Humble yourselves, therefore, under God's mighty hand, that he may lift you up in due time. 7 Cast all your anxiety on him because he cares for you.

2 Timothy 1:7 ; For the Spirit God gave us does not make us timid, but gives us power, love and self-discipline.

Deuteronomy 31:6 be strong and courageous. Do not be afraid or terrified because of them, for the LORD your God goes with you; he will never leave you nor forsake you."

1 Chronicles 28:20 David also said to Solomon his son, "Be strong and courageous, and do the work. Do not be afraid or discouraged, for the LORD God, my God, is with you. He will not fail you or forsake you until all the work for the service of the temple of the LORD is finished.

Psalm 56:3-4

When I am afraid, I put my trust in you. 4 In God, whose word I praise— in God I trust and am not afraid. What can mere mortals do to me?

Isaiah 41:10 so do not fear, for I am with you; do not be dismayed, for I am your God. I will strengthen you and help you; I will uphold you with my righteous right hand.

Isaiah 41:13 ; for I am the LORD your God who takes hold of your right hand and says to you, do not fear; I will help you.

Isaiah 54:4 ; "Do not be afraid; you will not be put to shame. Do not fear disgrace; you will not be humiliated.

You will forget the shame of your youth and remember no more the reproach of your widowhood.

1 Corinthians 16:13 ; be on your guard; stand firm in the faith; be courageous; be strong

1 Peter 3:13-14 ; who is going to harm you if you are eager to do well? 14 But even if you should suffer for what is right, you are blessed. "Do not fear their threats; do not be frightened."

Recite these words and tell fear, you are able to conquer it.

You will feel empowered and charged with words that can

lift your spirit. If you are not spiritual, there are

motivational words and quotes that can be used to move

past fears. It is said that the tongue has not bones but the

power it possesses through words can break a person.

Positive thoughts enhance confidence and confidence shifts

perspective and mindset. This can make a person more

productive.

Quotes on fears, if preferred to the biblical version,

"I learned that courage was not the absence of fear,

but the triumph over it. The brave man is not he who

does not feel afraid, but he who conquers that fear."
— Nelson Mandela

"Do one thing every day that scares you." — Eleanor Roosevelt

"There is only one thing that makes a dream impossible to achieve: the fear of failure." — Paulo Coelho

"I must not fear. Fear is the mind-killer. Fear is the little-death that brings total obliteration. I will face my fear. I will permit it to pass over me and through me. And when it has gone past I will turn the inner eye to see its path. Where the fear has gone there will be nothing. Only I will remain." — Frank Herbert, Dune

"Don't be afraid of your fears. They're not there to scare you. They're there to let you know that something is worth it." — C. JoyBell C.

"Don't give in to your fears. If you do, you won't be able to talk to your heart." — Paulo Coelho

"Nothing in life is to be feared, it is only to be understood. Now is the time to understand more, so that we may fear less." — Marie Curie

Chapter Five

CONFIDENCE BOOSTING

TACTICS

"Cowards die many times before their deaths; the valiant

never taste of death but once.

Of all the wonders that I yet have heard, It seems to me

most strange that men should fear;

seeing that death, a necessary end,

Will come when it will come." — William Shakespeare,

Julius Caesar

Change the only constant!

Everyone wants to improve certain aspect or aspects of their lives. There is always an area to improve on. It could be in our professional life, to earn a promotion or in our personal lives, to be loved. We want to feel essential and more importantly noticed as an essential person by others. Although, the desire to be valued is high, even higher is our hesitant energy. We are charged and willing and then suddenly, we are not. We hesitate, then procrastinate and never accomplish goals. Think about the goals you have set. Think about how energized you felt initially and then that voice in your head says _____ 'that is great! But I can never do that."

Think and reflect on what you were so excited about at the beginning of the year? A resolution perhaps, are you still excited or has the zeal changed? Was there a voice internally that told you to stop or that you cannot achieve it? So, how do we mute this voice? How do we talk over this silent voice in our head that is contrary to our goals? If we do not talk it down, then our confidence level will remain low. Below are some common tricks that can help boost our confidence and charge us to act.

1) Power Posture

While we do not want to walk around like superman or wonder woman with arms on the waist, walking tall helps. We still want to stand tall, straightened shoulders and maintain a straight posture. When you sit or stand with your shoulders straightened, you are not giving a sloppy look. You will feel empowered and confident. When you feel confident and stand confidently, you exude an overall confidence with your presence.

The universities of Columbia and Harvard conducted a research on body posture. It found that a confident body demeanor actually affects the chemical balance in our bodies. Specifically:

> The research was conducted on 42 students. *First, a saliva sample was taken from each subject and his or her testosterone and cortisol levels were measured. Second, the subject was asked to sit in either a "high-power" pose or a "low-power" pose for two minutes. Third, a second sample of saliva was taken from each subject and his or her testosterone and cortisol levels were measured again. The results showed that high-power poses increased testosterone by 20 percent (which boosts confidence) and decreased cortisol levels by 25 percent (which reduces anxiety).*

This means that we should make conscious efforts to balance our posture.

2) Chant and Affirm

Positive affirmations are great, incantations are awesome.

Practice both daily. And incantation can be a spiritual. It is

a focused directional energy chant. Merriam Webster

defines incantation as "a use of spells or verbal charms

spoken or sung as a part of a ritual of magic; also: a written

or recited formula of words designed to produce a

particular effect." Dictionary.com defines "incantation as

"the chanting or uttering of words purporting to have

magical power. " While dictionary. Com defines

affirmations as "the act or an instance of affirming; state of

being affirmed or the assertion that something exists or is

true". There are many ways to perform incantations and

affirmations that serve dual purposes in our lives.

Dual benefit incantation and affirmation steps:

- *Engage in a physical activity while chanting your incantations or confidently affirming your goals (Gardening, walking, exercising, jogging, dancing etc.)*
- *Know your focus and think only on your focus point to successfully attain it. Be specific for instance, say "I want to earn 30,000 additional salary" or "I want to be more confident when speaking at a work event" etc.*
- *Align your incantations with your beliefs (religions) and values (spiritual). Say what you mean and need and focus on that only. Do not be distant in your thoughts.*
- *Get emotional as you chant. Feel it as you speak it out.*
- *Meditate internally on your goal and chant it repeatedly*
- *Focus and chant for over 10minutes to get the greatest impact. Your energy increases as you chant more on your specific goal.*
- *Know what you want your outcome to look like!*

3) *Embrace Certainty*

Napoleon Hill said, "You've got to be sure of yourself before you can ever win a prize." Likewise Tony Robbins, is quoted as saying, "If you want to take the island, burn the boats!" He explained that if you do not burn the boats when things get rough, which likely, they would, you would retreat easily because the boat is readily available. There is safety in retreating which is appealing. This backup plan hinders progress. It reduces the intensity of action to achieve goal. When the boats are "burnt" the mindset shifts. There is no longer a fight or flight option, just fight. With the mindset shift, the desired goal becomes of victory and not escape.

What are your metaphorical "boats" that need to be burnt to allow success? Is there a safety net that you hold on to? Have you established that a life of mediocrity is okay? Have you told yourself you aren't _____ (fill in the blank: "smart," "pretty, "good", "Strong", "young," "old: etc.) enough to reach your goals? What opinions are you holding on to that are allowing you to sabotage your vision? Let go of those beliefs. Think positively. Focus on one option only-Success.

4) Jump to action

"Never confuse movement with action." Ernest Hemingway

"You can't build a reputation on what you are going to do." Henry Ford

Dale Carnegie said, "Action breeds confidence. If you want to conquer fear, do not sit at home and think about it. Go out and get busy!"

Confidence will not walk to you, neither will the uncertainly leave willfully. We will have to take action and with each action, uncertainly will lose its grip on us. Our confidence will get a boost. Self-confidence will bloom with each and every action we take. So we must Act! We need to do things and do new things, learn and gain confidence in self. Ask the four simple questions below to gain awareness and act:

What is your comfort zone?

What will I do today that is not within my comfort zone?

What is my biggest hurdle?

What daily steps am I taking to overcome that hurdle?

Do not expect perfection at your first try. It is better to try and fail, than to do nothing at all. Nevertheless, think positive that you will try and pass. Consistently taking action will gain you momentum and build confidence level within you. Florence Nightingale said, "You ask me why I do not write something.... I think one's feelings waste themselves in words, they ought all to be distilled into actions and into actions which bring results." Remember that action is essential to accomplishment and like Norman Vincent Peale noted, "Action is a great restorer and builder of confidence. Inaction is not only the result, but the cause, of fear. Perhaps the action you take will be successful; perhaps different action or adjustments will have to follow. But any action is better than no action at all."

Chapter Six

OBLIGATORY FOCUS

"Mind over matter represents the triumph of will over

physical hindrance. Our thoughts are our weapon against

the world."

— David Adam,

The debate between acting and not are always happening in our subconscious mind. We rarely agree with our brain when the mind and heart are involved. This can be seen when people are in love. We read about these popular wealthy and smart celebrities engaged in a messy divorce that costs them so much, financially and emotionally. We often wonder who in their right mind does that. Why would you risk everything you have worked so hard to achieve? Where are their advisers and /or lawyers? Why would anyone let them get married without signing a prenuptial agreement? We are filled with many questions to ask. The truth is, at the time, their brain knew they needed to have a good prenuptial agreement but their mind/heart tells them otherwise. Often, our mind/heart wins' battles such as these, after all, it is just money, right? Often, predictable outcomes and issues demand a mindful approach. We are vulnerable when we think with our hearts and leave our minds out. We can be misled by thinking with emotions only, strike a balance between emotional and rational thinking.

Our time is a precious commodity. While it is non-tangible, it cannot be bought or replaced. We need to learn to block out distractors and distractions. These occur in relationships, money, opinion, time, age etc. Understand your vision and goals, these come first. If we remain persistent and determined with faith and trust we will succeed. Success will depend on time. How you manage your time, who you spend your time with and what you devote your time to. On a daily basis, we live to satisfy our needs and wants. Whatever we do is something that affects our time. We magnify and intensify any idea in our consciousness. Our beliefs become our reality. For instance, when we make a mistake, we assume the world is watching and judging us.

Identify with your desire. A positive mindset. It is easy to point out negatives, rather than positives. We know what we do not want and how we do not like to feel, perhaps because it is unpleasant. For instance, imagine a child who touches a hot stove surface and gets burnt. They will become hard wired to refrain from touching a hot stove in the future. They do not want to feel the pain. In the same thinking, imagine, if the child touched the stove and a candy bar appeared. They will always go back to touching that stove (hot or cold). Now, we all know what we do not want, do we know what we want specifically? Learn to recognize what you want rather than what you don't. When you know what you desire, you would have taken the initial step to gaining exactly what you desire.

Clarity on your want is non-negotiable. Understand if you are just interested or are committed to what you want. Once you know what you want. Ask and gain your why. Why do you want it? How will you go about getting it? Will it be satisfactory? Will you stay focused and committed to this want? Imagine you get exactly what you want, are you satisfied? Gaining a clear picture of what you want and what it looks like, will keep you focused on your want.

Move beyond procrastinating. Procrastinating causes stagnation, and every time, hour, day wasted reduces the time for attaining success. Take steps. They might be small but take deliberate steps daily towards your goal. Do not be afraid of failing. Many successful people have failed in one or more actions. The difference is, they kept taking deliberate steps to their goals. As Jeffrey Fry simply stated, "Every expert began as an amateur." An example can be seen in Sir James Dyson, British inventor and founder of the Dyson Company. He saw failure as an essential part of his success. Dyson invented his first Dual Cyclone vacuum cleaner, which hit stores in 1993, he spent 15 years creating 5,126 versions that failed before he made one that worked brilliantly well. The payoff was a multi-billion-dollar company known for its creativity and forward-thinking designs. We often procrastinate due to fear.

Understand that Fear and timidity cripple and paralyze. Joshua 1:6-7, Joshua 1:18, Joshua1:3, Luke 1:32

Ask yourself,

Am I passionate about the work?

Am I one of the world's best at doing this work?

Will the market compensate me well enough for it?

These steps apply to anyone seeking a new career path.

Do you have a plan?

Are you documenting your plan?

What is your accountability check? Do you have one?

How will you start and maintain focus on task accomplishment?

What is your distractor? (Social media)

When is your most productive time?

What motivates your to be productive?

It is a great start to have an idea. The brain holds on to so many tasks with our daily life that it will be inefficient to rely on the brain as the singular reference check. If you think about everything you do daily, I am certain you will agree. Hence, it is important and necessary to document our goal. Your goal, strategy, tactic and time-line should be documented. Write down what you have done, need to do and will do. Documenting helps us focus and prevents undue anxiety.

The time spend in documenting our actions will seem a waste initially but it will improve productivity.

Think about a person who goes to the supermarket with a grocery list. They walk effortlessly and are directional in the aisle they visit. They pick everything on their list and are out on the store. Now, imagine someone who goes to the grocery store without a shopping list. They walk through every aisle in an attempt to remember everything they needed. While doing this, they are adding things they want to their shopping cart. At the end, they have spent more time and money than anticipated. They bought things that were not needed but wanted, for whatever reason. They might have fallen for a marketing tactic used by the store.

Whatever the case, not writing down exactly what they want increased cost. Even more terrible, is that, this person who does not have a list, gets home and has forgotten to purchase the very item they needed. Now, they have to make a second trip to the store to purchase what they need. I am certain this time around, they will be fast. They are headed back, frustrated and tired but focused on what they need. They now understand that if they do not get that item, it will waste their time. Why go through this hassle at all, when a simple list could save all this hassle?

Think about it, more was lost. There was time and money lost, obviously but there was also fuel lost, energy wasted and additional wear and tear on the vehicle, assuming they were driving. The point is, a simple act that might seem time consuming will save time and increased efficiency.

Hopefully, the lesson was learned from this shopping experience. The next time they go shopping, they will take a shopping list. If saving time and money is important to them. It is important to note one's value. Some, would enjoy that experience. They would not view it as a waste of time or resources, especially if it was gratifying. This is OK! Everyone is not with the same values nor same goals. However, if time management is essential to getting your goals, then your mindset needs to shift. We learn from our mistakes but should also learn from the mistakes of others on similar path. This way, we save time and energy. There is not enough time in the day, week, or year to make all the mistakes that we as humans, can make. Learn from others. Their success might motivate you but their failures will inspire and spark you. "Time management is an oxymoron. Time is beyond our control, and the clock keeps ticking regardless of how we lead our lives. Priority management is the answer to maximizing the time we have." — John C. Maxwell

Chapter Seven

SHIFTING APPROACH

"If you spend your whole life waiting for the storm, you'll never enjoy the sunshine."— Morris West

Perfection is overrated

Personality plays a huge role in our expectations. Some people are perfectionist and will refine a process until they feel it is perfect. While this is not a bad thing, often the quest for perfection delays and/or prevents us from achieving tasks and goals. Sometimes, time wasted on "polishing" a task to make it perfect will result in an opportunity lost. Imagine that person who spent countless hours rehearsing on their speech only to miss the actual opportunity to present that perfectly rehearsed speech. Or a person who had a novel idea but spent time perfecting it and someone else puts it out, making their idea obsolete. Technology and science enables things to move faster than usual that we often waste time and efforts when we "perfect" our work.

Release yourself of the unwanted pressure. Nothing and no person is perfect. Spending time working on perfection is a waste. Take risks and learn to "jump" to do the things that need to get done. The need to pause will vanish. There will be no hesitation in your actions. Taking risks might lead to a loss but will increase creativity and give room for growth.

Aspire to Inspire

"Do as I say" is not always the practice that many perform. Who is watching you? Everything we do publicly is noticed and even copied by someone else. Imagine for a moment, a mother who seats and crosses her legs to the right. She has done this repeatedly without consciously making an effort. Then one day, she notices her daughter sits the exact same way.

Authenticity

The motivation to be "liked" often makes us act the same as everyone else. We are afraid to stand out and not conform to the "norm". By doing this singular act, we betray our true self. When we fully embrace out true self, we are more creative and inventive. We can bring **about changes and improvements.** There have been people who stepped out of the norm and got job offers just by being authentic and not using the "usual" methods.

A couple of examples are talented Alec Biedrzycki put his gift for music to beneficial use when he wrote a song called 'Hire Me' to find a job, uploading a cheesy video to YouTube in the hope that prospective employers would come across it and offer him work. While he had to put up with the usual offensive comments from haters and trolls, Alec's cheesy song worked its magic and he ended up being offered a job in marketing. Josh's eBay auction, with 600 job applications under his belt yet zero offers, high school graduate Josh Butler realized desperate times had called for desperate measures, so he decided to attract the attention of potential employees by auctioning himself on eBay back in 2011. The auction went viral, securing Josh several interviews. Fast-forward to 2016, and he now has a successful career as a FFA Broker in the City of London.

Gain and Maintain Control

The good aspect of being aware is the ability to control. When you recognize the problem, you are on the right path to change or eliminate the problem. When you feel in control, it gives a sense of confidence, reduces anxiety and increases overall well-being.

Regrets come when we wonder, "What if?" yet don't act. Don't wonder – take the dive.

Fulfilled life

Living life outside of our comfort zone creates a euphoric feeling. You are amazed at yourself for being able to confront your limitation and move past it. When you overcome your fear, you gain self-respect and adoration for your tasks ahead. Lasting success comes from the ability to always push pass our comfort zone. Most things that help us grow are uncomfortable. Change is a necessary aspect of growth but often resisted. Think of your change as a moth transforming to a beautiful butterfly.

Do not be too afraid that you resist growth and remain stuck in a failing circle. You will discover that you are smarter, more resilient and able than you assumed, when you get uncomfortable.

Ask yourself, when was the last time you really wanted to try something but you shied away? Next time you find yourself wavering, go for it. The reward (and the lessons learned) will be, without question, worth the risk.

Typical mind questions that cause procrastination:

The fear of appearing dumb

The fear of being judged

The fear of something new

The fear of lack of imagination

The fear of lack of focus

Not worthy enough

Emotional blockage

Spiritual Blockage

Not smart or skilled enough

Embarrassed or Ashamed

> *Who I think I am*

> *Who they think I am*

> *Who I want them to think I am*

There are many reasons why we are stuck with and not acting. If you do not want to flight, flee or be frightened just be aware!
Stop, breath and then act.

- **Create a success Board and document the following and more:**

Traits of a thriving person

- Setting scale for achievement (personal)
- Success activities that work for you
- Success as a continuous process
- Navigation skills
  - Find your path
  - Clarify aim and determine objectives
  - Work life balance – sort out priorities
  - Peer pressure_ does the support of others matter?
  - Achieving equilibrium
  - Challenges of gender
  - Small steps- focus on gradual progress
  - Sustaining Clarity- Keep focus
  - Maintaining routine

Define Success in your own terms

What is most important to you?

What does a successful life look like

to you?

Who do you admire most? What

about their life do you wish to emulate?

How much are you willing to

commit to attaining your goals?

How will you measure your success

level?

When will you consider your actions

successful?

Skill Enhancing Steps:

- Set stretch goals
- Get formal and informal mentors and coaches
- Communicate and share progress
- Collaborate on projects and tasks
- Encourage people to share ideas and knowledge
- Continuously assess opportunity and changes needed
- Create supportive learning environment
- Establish concrete learning process
- Get leadership that reinforces learning
- Get learning opportunities and give also
- Facilitate self-driven learning
- Reward self-driven learning
- Ensure formal and informal learning

Learning with the Feynman's technique

The foundation of Feynman's learning technique is this: Before you can explain something clearly, you must understand it fully. It consists of four simple processes:

1. Select a topic/Subject
2. Explain it to a child
3. Simplify
4. Repeat

This is a theory that anything can be learned if we are open and honest with ourselves. Every concept can be simplified especially when explaining to five-year-old. The goal is to get the concept to be as clean and concise as possible. Pretend that you are teaching a class of kindergartens.

Often when we use complicated verbiage, it is to attempt to hide a shortcoming in our own understanding. When we fully comprehend an idea, we can explain in simple terms.

Feynman Technique

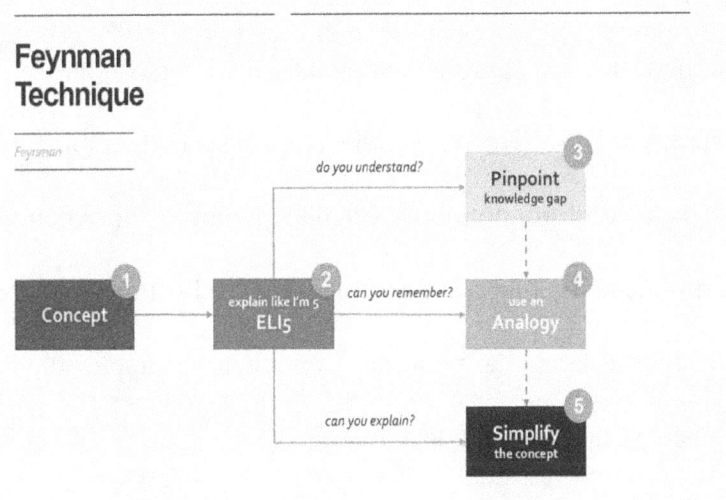

Examine your learning material more closely and fill in your knowledge gaps. If you struggle with the explanations, go back and read again.

Learn, relearn and repeat the learning for clarification. *That's it!* The Feynman technique is remarkably simple, which is why it's so effective. Concentrate on creating clear, simple explanations. You will understand and easily identify your business challenges. Learn a subject, immerse yourself in it and soon- you will be the subject matter expert. In 1960, a principle noted by the US navy, an acronym KISS (Keep it simple, stupid) stated that most systems perform optimally when kept simple rather than complicated. So, avoid unnecessary complications and keep designs as simple as possible. Same theory is applicable in business and personal teachings.

Chapter Eight
SORTING PRIORITIES

Eat the "Frogs" early:

It is a common saying to "eat that frog", which means to do your most difficult task first. When you do the most challenging task first, the pressure of spending the rest of your day thinking about those tasks is gone. For instance, I hate to work out, though I know I need to, however, when I do workout early in the morning, I am happy. On the days, I procrastinate, I spend all day thinking of when I can get on the treadmill or get a walk in, it is imbibed into all of my thoughts and affects my focus. Take care of your thoughts

Stress has an adverse effect.

Disruptive Innovation:

Be Flexible-:

Allow the space to tailor and refine your tactics and strategies to fit unmet needs. In today's ever changing world, the ability to adapt quickly is essential.

Be Unique-:

What are the things you do very well and do with your own style? If you do things in an unusual way that is productive and efficient then you have valuable and precious skills.

Be Open to learning-:

Knowledge is an essential tool in accomplishing task, however, there is more need to learn new and improved skills that will help accomplish tasks faster.

Identify a need-:

There are always needs that are not met. Sometimes people are aware and other times they are not. It is important to bring to "light" and unmet need.

Development Path:

Developing Performance-:

> Seek feedback and absorb the feedback. It will reveal areas of weaknesses that can be improved.

Expanded Network-:

> When you move pass your regular peers, you will learn more. Network with others outside your environment and learn more.

Helping others-:

> Training others will not only help them but help reinforce your knowledge and you might even learn new ones in the process. It is a give and take.

Coping and improving individual challenges-:

> The ability to manage complex situations, while minimizing anxiety levels and maximizing your performance level is invaluable.

PRACTICE DAILY HOW TO:

Help others

Be compassionate

Be Calm

Determined

Don't care about Naysayers

Pay attention to Inner Values

Meditate

Enhance Perception and Intelligence

Be conscious of your mortality- no time to do less than necessary (SADGHURU)

Change your preconceived notion

Work out routinely

QUESTIONS TO PONDER

Do you verbalize your thoughts?

If you did, what will it sound like?

Do you visualize your aspiration?

Do you rationalize your short comings?

Are you self-aware? Do you know what it means to be self-aware?

Do you work on autopilot?

What is your level of self-confidence?

Are you mostly Agreeable- Acceptance?

Are you determined?

Are there any aspects of developments you need?

Are you comfortable with your skills?

FOCUS TACTICS:

Document your goals, strategies and plan.

Review your goals, strategies and plan.

Revise, Implement, and Monitor progress

Revise or Change strategies as necessary.

Augment process

MINDSET MATTER

What is your mindset?

Implicit versus Explicit thinking

Interested or Committed versus Interested and committed

Are you aware of your conscious and unconscious mindset?

What are the influencers of your mindset? (Belief, assumptions, perceptions, desire, goal, purpose etc)

Gaining and excelling in a new skill requires change. A change in attitude and behaviors. Goal materialization require:

Focus, Clarity, Motivation, Strategies and Tactics

When we are self-aware, we can change our mindsets. We will take conscious efforts to alter out thinking patterns. Invest in yourself. Learning about your thinking habits and how to make them positive. Speak but more importantly think optimistic thoughts. Donald Trump, the 45th President of America had a positive mindset all though his campaign. When reviewing all his speeches and interview during the campaign, he always spoke with conviction, like he had won. He rarely used the word "if", he was always speaking on "when" and "what" he would do. Many wondered if he knew something already. Some even considered he'd rig the election. No. He drew success to himself.

The law of attraction. The "American dream", he embraced. He knew he was the only solution. Confidence and conviction, he attracted what he wanted. The simply law of physics. He became what he thought about, which was becoming the 45th President of the United States, with no prior experience. He spoke his position into existence, the universe stepped aside and let it happen. Albert Einstein said it eloquently as "Imagination is more important than knowledge. For knowledge is limited to all we now know and understand, while imagination embraces the entire world, and all there ever will be to know and understand."

Imagine yourself doing the things you want to accomplish. Like attracts like. See it, speak it and draw it to you. It is easy to visualize good things. Ask, believe and receive even when you do not know how nor are experienced. Believe in yourself and the universe will support you. When all seems to be going "awry", visualize the best outcome. It is not enough to want, see it, envision it, think about it and draw it to you! Just like we are "what we eat", we are what we think. Do not let negativity consume your thoughts, it is too expensive.

A funny thing happened on my birthday. A friend and I went to the casino. Immediately we sat down to play the quarter slot machine, I said, "I am going to lose, this will waste my money". And she turned around and said "Shhhhhh, we will win! Positive thinking". Do you want to guess who won at the end of the night?

Yes! She won some money. And I lost all my money. I caught myself thinking it and immediately I said it out, I wanted to give myself a good kick. It is not easy to think positively when our brains are wired to "protect" us. It takes practice, awareness and practice. I learned a valuable lesson.

Confront your fear based feelings

Are you considered a pessimist or an optimist? If you are always thinking about how bad life is, then chances are you are a pessimist.

STYLE AND APPROACH

We are often so busy in the day that we do not realize that we are truly controlled by our thoughts. Our thoughts direct our steps. When I bought my first car, a gray colored 1997 Honda Accord. It became the most popular car on the roads. Everyone was buying a 1997 Honda Accord. It was the latest and greatest car to be owned. Well, not really, but that was the story I told myself. Every time I looked around I saw a 1997 Honda Accord. More incredible was the fact that I would notice Gray 1997 Honda Accord vehicles everywhere I looked. Something in my inner thoughts was prompting me to only notice these specific car.

Without any effort, my thoughts were controlling my sight, perception and reality. I spoke to a colleague who was pregnant at the time. Her thoughts was that there were too many pregnant women that year. She felt everywhere she looked, she could spot at least one pregnant woman. The mind is constantly at work. This is why it is very important to control the mind. Humans are usually hard wired in similar functional capacity. Our thoughts translate into our actions and reactions. These actions and reactions shape the mindset of others around us.

If we are aware of our mindset and the way it works, then we are able to alter it to suit our needs. The mindset of an individual will provoke their responses to situations. Managing individual mindsets is imperative to attaining desired actions. External and internal factors shape our mindset. External factors such as culture, peers, parents, mentor, idols, etc. and internal factors such as feelings, beliefs, perceptions, etc.

The high achiever is always conscious and intentional in their actions. They purposely act and create activities that are geared towards influencing directly or indirectly how others think, feel and/or preform. There are three aspects of a mindset that will prompt a person to move beyond their comfort zone and act. The emotional intelligence mindset, rational action mindset and the growth mindset. Emotional intelligence will provide the skills required to inspire self and others. Rational action mindset will provide the skills necessary to connect and act. While the growth mindset allows for focus, accountability and action.

Mindsets are formed from varying experiences hence the differences in humans. Weekly, I go over the grades posted online with my two middle school children. Their countenance and responses are always opposite. The 8th grader is more anxious and the 7th grader calm. Both have one or two subjects where they are not performing at their optimal capacity. When I ask what can be done to improve the grades, the 8th grader is quick to provide suggestions while the 7th grade gives a nonchalant look. This is not as simple as blaming it on their culture and surroundings, both have been exposed to the same culture and surroundings. It is interesting how different they are responding.

I took the 7th grader into a room and asked what she was thinking. I was curious to know why she was so calm, when I clearly had been disappointed in her grades. I asked her , "Did she simply not care what I thought?" Her response was astounding. She said, she knew I was "all bark and no bite". I would get upset but will calm down soon and let them be. Clearly, she had formed her perception of what my responses would be. She felt confident in her ability to predict my actions. Her mindset was fixed. She was not going to change, agitate or motivate herself to impress me. Then, I understood that implicit thinking had prompted her external actions.

Chapter Nine

ROLE MODEL-CONSISTENCY

"Consistency is the hallmark of the unimaginative."

— Oscar Wilde

"Consistency is the true foundation of trust. Either keep your promises or do not make them."

— *Roy T. Bennett*

The foundation of any symbiotic relationship is trust. We model those we trust. Most of us strive to act like someone we admire. Children naturally in the early stages of their lives, admire their parents as their role models. Employees admire that hardworking and consistent manager or senior employee as a role model. Interns admire staff employees as role models. The idea is a role model is at a place we aspire to be. They are doing something that inspires others.

In other to practice and excel in what we do, we must not only act but remain steady in action. Think about the weight loss success stories told. Some who released a significant amount of weight usually gain them back when they relax. They stopped doing the things they did to get their success. Success attainment and continuation requires consistent actions.

Consistency is vital because knowingly or unknowingly we are shaping some other person's perception of us. I once spoke with a sales manager who could never get his team motivated. They had worked very well when the product first arrived. They had a good week when the new product first launched. Employees had been promised time off with pay if they sold a certain quantity. The employees then exceeded the sales required.

The management acknowledged their efforts, However the reward promised was not provided. The sales manager did not know how to allow all the employees enjoy time off with pay, which was initially promised. It was an expense that they could not afford at the time. Instead, he treated his employees to lunch that week. While the employees appreciated the lunch, they were not satisfied. This affected their morale.

I approached and spoke with one of the team members. I was curious at the turnaround in work ethic. I had taken it upon myself to enlighten the management on the reasoning behind the decline in employee morale. They had good will but their actions were inconsistent with their words. The team member explained that they felt cheated. On any other day, they will be grateful and satisfied with the lunch treat. In fact, the treat would have been sufficient to get the employees motivated. Their morale would have been high and efficiency at optimal level. They would be effective at their job and the goals would be attained or even exceeded.

Another situation with a friend who always promised her six year old son chocolate when he cleaned his room. She had promised to reward a positive action on his part. He cleaned his room the first week and then stopped. When I spoke with him. He stated, *"Mommy lied"*. *"Mommy promised chocolate, but gave me cookies, so, I*

decided not to clean my room until she gets my chocolate. "
I was amused.

The fact is inconsistency in behavior creates a perception that an individual is unpredictable. Being unpredictable severely impacts trust. People need trust to perform on an optimal level. A predictable and consistent individual is perceived as trustworthy. It is important to be perceived trustworthy, it makes others feel safe with you. As a role model, you want others to trust you. It allows them to share vital information with you. This is a trait to possess both in a professional and personal setting. Knowledge will be willingly shared with you.

Understand that willing or unwillingly, you are a role model to someone else. There are always people who look up to you therefore, do your best to be a good model. People will trust you to be logical, even in dire situations.

Consistency means that you are able to respond rationally. People will trust that you will not go overboard with your reaction when something bad happens. While you might be happy or not, your response and action will be indifferent when you are consistent. This takes practice and awareness. You are trusted to react with rational and non-threatening behavior when adversity occurs.

NURTURER

This is a quality that demonstrates your understanding and compassion towards others. People love to follow a nurturer. We naturally are wired to want to encourage others, especially someone younger. It's no wonder, many people are mentors and more companies are encouraging their senior level employees to mentor others. Even colleges are encouraging mentoring in schools.

It is hard to learn all that need to be learned, however,

through training others, you are also learning. It is a

refreshing experience. One that gives and receives. Often,

we do not take time to revise what we have learned,

however when we teach others, we learn.

Chapter Ten

HOP AND LEAP

"It is better to act and repent than not to act and regret."

— *Niccolò Machiavelli, the Letters of Machiavelli*

As the elevator sound beeped, Sola Edefe straightened his shoulder, used his hands to smooth down his beards and walked bravely out of the elevator. The elevator had opened right in front of the receptionist desk. "I got this" he muttered underneath his breath as he walked towards the receptionist. Sola could feel the sweat run down his armpit. He never perspired this much. Well, thank goodness, he thought as his mind races to an embarrassing moment in the past where he used too much cologne and had the interviewers coughing. He wondered if he had remembered to use his deodorant. Sola had been job hunting for over six months. This was going to be his first interview in a long time. Sola knew he was smart and capable, but he has just returned from Nigeria two years earlier. He had not worked a professional job for 5 years. With one semester to graduate, Sola's parents died in an automobile accident and Sola had to leave college to go back to Nigeria. He managed to graduate by taking his last class online while in Nigeria.

This interview meant everything to Sola and he worried about messing it up. Sola had studied Accounting and planned to work for one of the top five accounting firms. But, like it often happens, life intervened. Sola lost his parents and he had to organize estate matters. There was no room for work. Especially, not work at the other part of the world. Sola needed to organize the issues with his parent's assets and debts. He was their only child.

Returning back after 4 years, Sola worked on his certificate and passed. He became a Certified Public Accountant (CPA). He did some little work for friends and neighbors as a CPA. It felt good to earn some money. It allowed him to get some practice and re learn and train his brain. Now, he was ready to get a job with a top accounting firm. He was ready to make the big bucks!

Sola, worked odd jobs so he had something to put on his resume. He had been out of the professional field for so long that he didn't feel confident even as a junior accountant. His resume looked good with the CPA on it. However, the massive gap in the work experience sector was a concern. He did a lot with putting the estate together and organizing things in a chaotic environment like Nigeria. Was this something he could put on his resume, he wondered?

Maybe just speak to it and tie it to a response during the interview, he thought. Sola, needed to network, make small talk and promote himself. Sola was an introvert. He certainly did not enjoy networking and self-promoting. He felt his credentials should speak for themselves. He did not enjoy telling strangers about his wonderful talents, skills and abilities. He felt this was "showing-off" and even beyond not self-promoting, he did not enjoy imposition.

He did not want to be perceived as imposing

himself on others. This aspect of his personality, kept him from doing a lot of things. In fact it kept him up at night. He would compose emails and attached his resume but will desist from hitting the send button. He needed a job, he just did not want to impose. He felt it was "borderline begging" for attention and a job. Sola hated the feeling. It made his stomach churn and his heart race.

Sola was very uncomfortable because he was not self-assured in what he was selling. Sola, was always cognizant of his "accent". He had heard it too many times and almost always whenever he got talking. Surprisingly, he had even heard it in Nigeria. Everywhere he had been, someone always ask "I detect an accent" or "What country are you from?"etc. Sola could not control others but he tried to control his reactions. He worried because he felt this might impede his chances at an interview. Sola was determined. He would not let all this discomfort deter his determination.

Sola did not want to live in regrets. More importantly, he was tired of being broke. All these opinions were not going to feed his starving stomach. He had to remember how far he had come. He could use the stable income. It was clear to Sola when his finance' called informing him that her parents will not pay for their dream wedding. That one phone called changed Sola's self-doubt. He knew he had to move out of the way of his "feelings". It was time. He had to get a stable paying job. He needed steady income stream. The time was now.

Networking events proved to be predictable. He felt awkward. He would have to engage in positive self-talk and push himself before he could speak out. He took deep breaths repeatedly, as a relaxation technique. Surprisingly, when things got flowing and everyone was mingling, people were nice. No one noticed Sola's perspiration or accent and if they did, they simply ignored. Many focused and discussed his skills. One, he was proud to talk about freely. The generosity and kindness of people surprised Sola. He was glad he "jumped". Sola, had listened, read and memorize words from authors who talked about "jumping", "leaping", getting off comfort zone for growth etc.

Sola's prior experience gave him this uncomfortable feeling that he would not be received well. He wondered how he would walk into an office of well dressed "strangers" and sell himself. Would they think he was a complete waste of their time? These are busy people. Here he was at a professional networking event with these top executives and staff. There were all levels of professionals at the event and most were nice. His expectations were completely wrong. People were nurturing, caring and generous. They did not seem to mind talking to him. They could understand his "accent". They did not act irritated or diminutive with him. Sola actually enjoyed the experience. Who knew! He did not think he would enjoy meeting and connecting with people. He enjoyed networking and talking about job opportunities. This was a big aha moment for him. He wondered if he had applied this strategy, he possibly could have grown his business largely. What he had dreaded all this while was actually really enjoyable. He had a good time networking and showcasing his skills.

The receptionist greeted Sola warmly. She was nice. Sola, knew she got paid to be nice but he also felt valued which added to his confidence. She informed him that the interviewers will be with him in a few minutes. Sola took a seat. He wondered why interviewers always made people wait for so long, when he arrived on time. He began to hear his inner voice speak negatively. He quickly changed that negative thought to only positive thoughts. He kept praising and boosting his skills in his thoughts. He rehearsed in his head, all his skills. Sola wondered about coming off condescending but he quickly laughed it off. Nothing was wrong with confidence. When called into the interview, about twenty minutes later, Sola was prepared. Sola walked into the interview feeling confident in his abilities and skills. He was offered the job on the spot and with more salary than he expected.

Nothing to Lose

"You are what you do, not what you say you'll do."
— *C.G. Jung*

A relaxed attitude is needed. While you do not want to be perceived as haughty, you do not want to be perceived as ordinary either. You will discover her liberating it is when you do that thing you once feared first. As Brian Tracy wrote in his book, Eat that frog, "If you have to eat two frogs, eat the ugliest one first. "This is another way of saying that if you have two important tasks before you, start with the biggest, hardest, and most important task first."

When you do what seems the hardest, you will realize that everything else becomes easier. Think about the first time you took a cruise, or ate an exotic cuisine or traveled to a new destination. It is a scary feeling trying anything new. There are many feelings clashing within us. What "ifs", such as what if I do not like it but what if I do? The clash of the "angel" and the "devil" within all of us.

One thought is giving good vibes and the other bad. We are not sure which to believe. This is why we need to shift out mindset to a "nothing to lose" mindset. If you were hungry anyway, then eating that new meal will help and if you taste and do not like it, some waiters will exchange your meal, so what do you have to lose trying it out? And if the vacation to a new destination is enjoyable, then you go your money's worth and gained and experience. If you do not like the destination, then you gained an experience and knowledge. It is a matter of how much you gain. Refrain from thinking about a loss.

Certainly, there will be some situations that will be stressful and difficult. Situations that simply thinking positively seem ineffective. So many experiences, personally and otherwise, reveal there is something positive in trying new things. The drive for doing something out of our regular lifestyle makes this "jump" powerful. Taking "jumps" lead to extraordinary self-discovery. The idea all hinges on "jumping". The common saying of "look before you leap" will not help you discover your additional strengths and abilities.

Go after what you need. The time spent "looking" will stop you from acting. Avoidance is used to stunt growth. When we avoid a situation because of the challenges, either professionally or personally, we do not grow. Instead, we allow fear, worry, and self-doubt keep us from our dream life. When we gather up the courage to try it, it may be quite a surprising and enlightening discovery.

This was certainly the case for Cordelia Sosa, a timid, shy and reserved young lady. She was nominated as the student body president at her final year in college. She knew she would have to "campaign" for everyone else to vote her in. She had been put in a tight position. She did not want to let those who nominated her down but also she did not want to appear incompetent to those she was soliciting their votes. She would have to knock on doors and speak to strangers. She would need to gain constituents, begging, engaging and convincing them to like her and her values.

She needed to market herself. She dreaded self-promotion but this was a skill that was essential for this task. She always loved politics. She was grateful for the nomination but she was not certain of her abilities. Cordelia was a diffident person with little social aptitude. She dreaded any spontaneous and unrehearsed conversations with strangers.

Now, she no longer had to get used to spontaneity but she had to learn and engage in selling herself. She had to become the "product" or "commodity" that needs to be marketed. She was to be the first line marketer! It almost felt intolerable and excruciating to consider. All these thoughts seemed like this opportunity was a waste but there was an appeal about this opportunity that kept her interested.

Cordelia wanted to make a difference. She loved community work with charitable organizations. She used any opportunity she got to speak up for student benefits and improvement of the campus. She had always been inspired by stories of public servants. The philanthropists, politicians, legislators, mayors, governors etc. She could identify with the things that made them contest and/or act. Her desire to make a difference will only be possible in a platform where her reach was extensive. She would be able to reach a wider audience and provide support needed, to more people. It made logical sense and she was going to suppress her emotional side.

Cordelia went for it. Surprisingly, she enjoyed the process. It was time consuming, exhausting and unpredictable but she enjoyed it all! The amount of people she spoke to weekly overwhelmed her on some days during the campaign. Though exhausting, she learned from the conversations. She found them to be valuable. Many of the conversations validated Cordelia's reasons for getting into public service.

Fascinatingly, she gained more knowledge when she communicated with others. In the famous words of Kenneth H. Blanchard, "None of us is as smart as all of us" She would often avoid self-promoting when she needed to learn. People reacted positively when they felt genuinely cared about. The magic happened when people were encouraged to "vent". Many talked about their struggles. A wide range of issues from financial aid, housing to curriculum etc. Cordelia won the election and was able to make a difference in the lives of the students during her tenure. More importantly, she had accomplished a scary adventure and it turned out to be growth and skill procurement for Cordelia.

There will be a point that we all have to make a decision to "jump" or stay "stuck". You will get moments to "jump", a defining moment. And you will recognize this opportunity by the "fear" and uncertainty you feel. Please understand that you might be pleasantly surprised by the opportunities opened when you "jump".

Attending a networking event can be a terrifying experience for some, especially when they do not know anyone there. Uncertain of the best approach to promote yourself, display your talent and/or market your skills. In fact you dread getting into small talks with strangers. Your fears are keeping you "stuck". Zig Ziglar wrote, "F-E-A-R has two meanings: 'Forget Everything and Run' or 'Face

Everything and Rise.' The choice is yours." Choose the latter and act. You will be glad you did. Everyone feels fear but not everyone allows fear to cripple them. Remain aware and push fear to the side and achieve what you need.

It is OK to feel awkward beeping your own horn but do it anyway. Most people do not want to be viewed as "shallow" or conceited, But in the words of K. Blanchard, "If you don't blow your own horn, someone else will use it as a spittoon. " If you do not do it, no one else will for it for you and no one will recognize your great ability. If it is critical for your success and growth, then it must be done. It is not an option. When you are sick and tired of being stuck in the same place with no growth, you will do it. If you have to speak with a large audience and you are terrified of doing this. Start small but begin with any opportunity that avails itself, for instance in church, social gathering, meetings etc. It is important and necessary. This is why the importance of positive self-talk cannot be ignored. When you start small, you have the opportunity to practice. If you make a mistake, it is OK. You are human and will be better able to connect with the audience.

Embrace looking like a "fool". We are often afraid of speaking up because we do not want the criticism. As you walk into a building to network or present, imagine you just said the best thing possible and everyone is applauding you. This will boost your confidence. You will speak clearly. The story in your head is that you are doing wonderfully hence you are putting out your best.

American actor, comedian, rapper, songwriter and producer, Will Smith recently went skydiving with his friends in Dubai and spoke candidly about his experience. His actions that defied his fear. His anxiety and panic experience after making the commitment to skydive with friends.

He talked about his terrifying experience about skydiving. He recounted how he was restless the previous night. In addition, he talked about the terrifying experience of going to the site. He did not want to be mocked by his friends, hence he found the courage to go anyway. Knowing he was highly terrified.

His fear was real but he did it anyway. The instructor has pushed him off on the count of two, though he was expecting the count of three. The reason was that people, given a chance, will always take the easy way out. Yes, the instructor said, jump when I count to three but he had also observed that people resist the urge to jump at three. Hence the reasoning for pushing at two. Sounds logical, our brains are wired to resist danger.

However, once he was pushed Will Smith experienced the other side of his fear. He "realized it was the most blissful experience. At the point of maximum danger is the point of minimum fear. It is bliss. On the other side of our terror are the best things in life." The point of these stories are that, when you "jump", you start to experience and see things with new eyes.

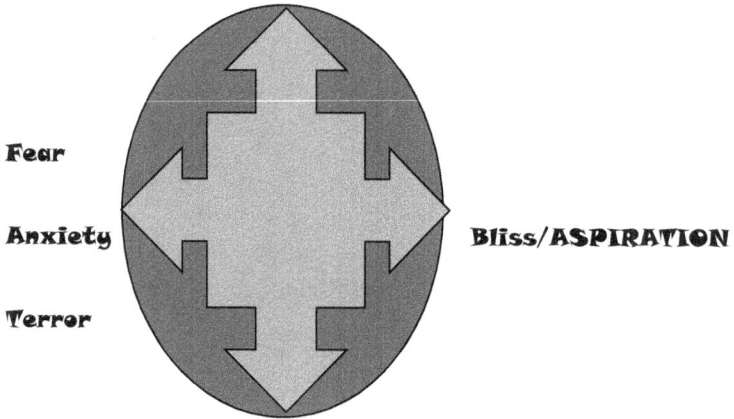

Fear

Anxiety   Bliss/ASPIRATION

Terror

Steps to practice when moving from comfort zone:

- Set extravagant goals

- Solicit formal and informal mentors and coaches in the same Professional and\or personal path

- Communicate, teach and share progress

- Collaborate on projects and tasks

- Encourage people to share ideas and knowledge

- Continuously assess opportunity and changes needed

- Define supportive learning environment

- Establish concrete learning process

- Get leadership that reinforces learning

- Get learning opportunities and give also

- Enable self-driven learning

- Reward self-driven learning

- Ensure formal and informal learning

Chapter Eleven

CIRCADIAN RITUALS (Avoid or Add)

There is a discomfort that we experience when doing something outside our norm. When you gain clarity on your purpose and conviction on your skill-set then you will customize your daily rituals. Unknowingly our rituals also add to our anxiety. What are we avoiding versus what we should be adding? If we add little positive actions to our daily lives, we will be closer to our goals. Think about a task or behavior you always avoid doing. What are the simple additions you can add?

I remember speaking with a friend, whom I had not seen in two years. She looked wonderful. She had lost a tremendous amount of weight. She looked radiant. It felt like she had reversed aging. In my typical curious nature, I asked, "What did you do?" My eyes were wide open, head tilted down and arms wide open waiting for a hug. She explained that she did not do anything special. She had always wanted to release the weight but was never able to commit to doing the things required.

Instead, she committed to adding one healthy behavior to her life. This was easier for her, shifted her mindset and solved her problem at the same time. She said, "I started with water". I would drink a gallon of water daily unfailingly. This was going to be my new way of life. Then she reduced her meat intake after the third month. When she got used to that, she added a daily five-minute dumbbell exercise.

She went on and one about the trivial things she did over that time that have now become a part of her. We eat daily and move daily, so why not add our own variation to what we would do daily anyway. This was her mindset. She did not think of it as a "diet", which she coined as "die yet" nor did she think about it as a lifestyle change. She simply just called it additions and variations of my life. Here is when I say, "Whatever works!" What we do daily will always change us overtime. It takes tiny actions to get massive results but the key is consistency.

Maintaining that simple behavior always. Often we realize that the task that seemed so impossible or difficult is not so bad after all. We feel empowered that we can do it. Our anxiety diminishes and we likely engage in that activity again. Again, with the story of Will Smith Skydiving, he talked about taking both his sons to skydive also. He wanted his children to have the experience he had.

However, he also decided to skydive straight, a variation of his initial dive. One that allowed him to fall faster and scarier. He wanted to land first which would allow him to see his children as they descended from their dive. This was a lesson in practice in addition. He had added this aspect to his experience. He experienced bliss with the initial sky diving but this was different. So, he subjected himself to gaining that same feeling, acting with fear. Take control of your subconscious thoughts and act.

Imagine what you could do if you did not get stuck on perceived scrutiny from friends and family? How far would you go with your ideas and goals if fear did not inhibit you? There is always that internal voice that causes us to second guess our instinct to act. Learning how to silence it is possible with daily practice.

Routinely practice doing the opposite of what that voice is saying. It can be as simple as mowing your lawn or working out. When you think about working out and the voice says, "You cannot work out, you are too tired" or "your feet hurt's you cannot work out", then workout, same is applicable if it was mowing the lawn. There are always opportunities in our daily lives to practice doing the opposite of our natural fear and avoidance instinct.

Chapter Twelve

AUTHENTICITY-You did that!

"Being confident and believing in your own self-worth is

necessary to achieving your potential."

— *Sheryl Sandberg*

The truth is perception is the reality of the owner. People react and act based on their level of discernment. It is important that you conduct yourself with sincerity and honesty. Be yourself and treat people accordingly. In order to "be yourself", you need to become aware with who you truly are! Dedicate some time to getting to know yourself. We evolve daily, based on our experiences and if we are not aware, then we might not be acting with authenticity.

Confidence is an essential part of success. You can build confidence by being authentic. Confidence allows you to grow. You will stretch beyond and extend your abilities, skills and focus. It allows you to open capabilities you didn't know existed within.

Confidence is a teachable and learn-able skill. The more we practice things, the more confident we are in showcasing it. If a person feels incompetent or lacks the knowledge to train others, they will shy away from opportunities. If this same person, were to learn and be taught extensively, they will seek out opportunities to teach what they know. So, lack of knowledge -----Shy away and full of knowledge ---------Seek out opportunities. There is a solid correlation between knowledge and confidence.

Lack of confidence usually is the result of lack of awareness and ability. In some instances, it might be emotional or cultural in nature. It is easy to train the brain to boost confidence when it is due to a lack of awareness and knowledge. What gaps need to be filled? What will you need to learn to feel confident? Is the atmosphere conducive?

Further exploring the adventure of Will Smith's Sky diving experiencing that occurred twice, he did what he never thought he could and repeated it! Sheryl Sandberg in her book, Lean in, wrote "Done is better than perfect". Perhaps Will Smith was not confident in his ability to skydive, but he did it anyway. In doing this singular act, he earned more trust among his friends.

What started off as an interest among friends talking, while drinking, quickly turned into a commitment when they agreed on a time, place and day. It would have been easy for anyone of the friends to brush the idea aside. They did not do that, they all responded and affirmed their commitment. In anything we do, we must realize that sticking to a commitment   makes us more appealing. To remain an authentic person who has integrity, you should do what your commit to.

An authentic person is likely to seek assistance where needed. They will be confident in their skills and gain knowledge to become competent. Competence builds confidence which is a critical aspect of moving through our comfort level. Being confident will help unlock potentials. Potentials known and unknown, this is due to the creativity and innovative aspect correlated with heighten confidence.

Confidence allows us to act at our best. We are efficient and effective when we are confident. A confident individual is also able to influence people around them. It is an asset to an individual and a company when a person is confident. They are able to

Act with pride

Showcase skills

Engage self and others in positive outputs

Connect easily with others

Collaborate and team promote

AUTHENTIC CONNECTION

Ever wondered why you meet some people and you seem to instantly connect with them? If you think deeper, you might realize the many similarities you both possess. There are also certain variables such as mutual respect, appreciation, and awareness. Connections are instant or built over time. A common trait among leaders is their ability to connect with the multitude of people they meet daily.

The skill, desire and poise to put their energy into connecting with others is visibly noticeable.

Pause and think: Most leaders that connect easily always use names when introducing themselves and in turn ask for your name (phonetic pronunciation if an unusual name, like mine). The point is they show a keen interest in learning about you and most will remember you by name the next time they meet you.

Think of most politicians, can you notice how easily they connect with people? They possess innate charisma. The 44th president of the United States of America, Barack Obama and his wife, Michelle, as an example, excelled at connecting with people quickly. In addition, there is also Bill and Hillary Clinton, Ronald Reagan and even celebrities like Oprah Winfrey, Maya Angelou, Will Smith and many others. While it might be easy to interact with others, the ability to truly connect with others come from being a genuine person. It has nothing to do with IQ (Intelligence quotient) but rather EQ (Emotional quotient) and emotional intelligence. Regardless of your status, politician, celebrity, athlete, family member etc. This is a skill that can be learned. Yes, some are born with it but others can work to achieve this skill. The art of being able to win people's trust is more essential than being book smart.

How do we recognize the need for this skill? Think about who and what you focus on during a conversation. Most people who genuinely connect in a conversation or meeting are always focused on the other person. This will take some practice especially if it is not a natural habit. For instance, as a native of Washington, and obviously a fan of Washington Wizards, I may not like the Boston Celtics very much, but the brilliance of Isaiah Thomas cannot be denied. People like Isaiah Thomas because he can form an authentic connection. Switching from talkative mode to listening mode changes everything. All our communication efforts goes into understanding. We are able to understand the content and intent of the person we are communicating with. After listening intently, we are able to speak coherently and precisely. We are able to be effective, concise and accurate with our responses. We are now able to speak efficiently and get our audience to be at their maximum listening capacity.

Practice tips to gain trust in communication;

Speak at a comfortable location

Stay focused on your audience

Greet your audience warmly

Start the connection with a human connection (handshake, hug, etc.) not a functional one

Add humor and humility

Positive Affirmations

I am awesome/able/amazing/attractive/adored/admired/astounding

I am brace/bold/beautiful/beaming/bright/bountiful/better

I am calm/cool/confident/considerate/charming/captivating

I am daring/determined/dedicated/decisive/decent/dazzling/dashing

I am effective/efficient/energetic/empathy/eloquent/enviable

I am Fun/Fantastic/favored/fulfilled/full/flowing/fabulous

I am Generous/gallant/glorified/glamorous/great

I am
Honest/happy/harmonious/hardworking/humble/hale/hearty

I am
Imaginative/Ingenious/inspired/inventive/important/impecc able/incredible

SELF DISCOVERY PRACTICE

Professional Assessment

What areas would be ideal to improve on for work?

Self-promotion for a raise, bonus, conference o, recognition etc.

Speaking up at team meetings

Giving training and seminars

Receiving and /or giving negative feedback

Seeking additional help or support

Communication with seniors/executives

Accountability

Flexibility

Personal Assessment

Attending a party where you do not know a lot of people

Getting into a difficult conversation with a close friend or family member

Making small talk at a networking event

Speaking at a public event

These are some examples and not applicable to everyone. It is better to customize your list based on your challenges and/or experiences.

Use these ratings in answering the questions below- Be sincere with yourself

1= Agree

2=Strongly Agree

3= Neutral

4=Disagree

5=strongly disagree

Knowledge reflection assessment

_____1. *I am very knowledgeable about the task needed in this situation*

_____2. *I do not feel confident in my knowledge of the task*

_____ *Total Knowledge Score*

Authenticity reflection assessment

_____1. *I am comfortable performing the task as myself*

_____2. *I feel strange performing these tasks.*

_____ *Total Knowledge Score*

Competence reflection assessment

_____1. *I am competent and able to complete these tasks*

_____2. *I feel confident performing these tasks.*

_____ *Total Knowledge Score*

Congeniality reflection assessment

_____*1. I am sure people will like me in this situation*

_____*2. I am not worried that people will be turned off from me in this situation.*

_____ *Total Knowledge Score*

Morality Reflection Assessment

_____*1. I worry about being ethical and logical*

_____*2. I have concerns about my morality when in this situation*

_____ *Total Knowledge Score*

Take a look at your scores. Where are your challenges? Where did you rank highest and lowest?

Note the aspects that are challenges and note the aspects that aren't so challenging.

Self-Awareness reflections

What would people rate you as in sincerity on a scale of 1-10?

Do you need to be cared for at work and at home?

Would people describe you as one who gets irritated and frustrated often?

What would your acquaintances score you (rate out of 10)?

Recall a recent example of your sincere actions

Provides two examples of authenticity, either at work or home.

Identify the role models and the influencers in your life

Study these individuals and consider how they have shaped your behavior

Are there similar traits? List the traits that are similar and different.

Gain Clarity on your decision making process. Often we make a decision against our gut instincts because we "jump". We act before our mind has a chance to catch up with our actions.

What is the circumstances surrounding your "jump" or lack thereof?

Chart the best case scenarios if you do "Jump"

Chart the worst case scenarios if you do "Jump"

Chart the best case scenarios if you do not "Jump"

Chart the worst case scenarios if you do "Jump"

Self-Analysis

Nuisances in Mindset

List your top ten irritants in mindsets. What are the specific things that will deter you from learning to change your mindset? Be specific in your description and with the exact contexts. Using an example to describe your point might help properly express your point. For instance, is there someone who is always nice and you think they are being "phony" because it is not possible for a person to be that "nice" all the time?

1._____
_____

2._____
_____

3._____
_____

4._____
_____

5._____
_____

6._____
_____

7._____
_____

8._____
_____

9._____

_____

10._____

_____

ASK- Questions to assist in understanding your Mindset.

How do people rate their level of understanding you? Do they perceive you as easy to understand?

What impact do you have on others (Professionally and personally?)

How willing are you to help others genuinely?

Do you understand the impact you have on others?

How self-aware are you?

Are you deliberate or Reactive?

What is your level of empathy? (High, medium or low)

Do you understand your responsibility?

Do you procrastinate? (Self-esteem, doubtful, fear of judgment etc)

Do you act fairly to all? (Emotional or rational)

Are you perceived as trustworthy, consistent and fair?

MUST- Specific actions that need to be done.

Be brutally honest

Make a commitment

      To change

      To learn

To follow through to completion

Identify your interest and your commitment.

Stop the Negative self-talk and sabotage.

Expand Skills and Expertise. (Ignorance is not bliss)

SKILL- Knowledge and learning

How to make money in business.

1) Increase your self-worth by increasing your activity (learning and working)

Set financial goal based on what you want not what you think you can get

Write down all the reason why you want that financial goal

Is this a short term or long term goal?

Set goal and figure out your strategy and tactic

2) Learn how to manage money

You have to be accountable with your money. It is one thing to make money and another to have money. When you make money and do not know how to manage that money, you will have none. Learn to live within your means. Do not live above your means. Spend less than you earn.

Do not spend based on expected earnings, spend based on current earnings minus your bad debt. You have to learn discipline. Jim Rohn said "We must all suffer from one of two pains: the pain of discipline or the pain of regret. The difference is discipline weighs ounces while regret weighs tons." What is the pain you are willing to endure?

3) Learn to invest and save money

Determine your goals and values. If you are not a risk taker then invest safely with just a savings account but understand, you will not become wealthy doing this. Are you able to learn skills that will assist you in investing?

INSPIRATIONAL QUOTES

"Never was anything great achieved without danger."

— Niccolò Machiavelli

"All courses of action are risky, so prudence is not in avoiding danger (it's impossible), but calculating risk and acting decisively. Make mistakes of ambition and not mistakes of sloth. Develop the strength to do bold things, not the strength to suffer." — Niccolò Machiavelli

"Only if you know to what extent your logic should go and where it should not go, your life will be beautiful." — Sadhguru, Mind is your Business

"If you're offered a seat on a rocket ship, don't ask what seat! Just get on." — Sheryl Sandberg

"Done is better than perfect." — Sheryl Sandberg

"Never confuse movement with action." — Ernest Hemingway

"Action expresses priorities." — Mahatma Gandhi

"By three methods we may learn wisdom: First, by reflection, which is noblest; second, by imitation, which is easiest; and third by experience, which is the bitterest."
— Confucius

It does not matter how slowly you go as long as you do not stop." — Confucius

"The man who moves a mountain begins by carrying away small stones." — Confucius

"Attack the evil that is within yourself, rather than attacking the evil that is in others."
— Confucius

"I hear and I forget. I see and I remember. I do and I understand."
— Confucius

Carol Kinsey Goman in her article for Forbes

magazine noted

12 body poses that boost confidence:

1. Stand tall and take up space. Power, status, and confidence are non-verbally displayed through the use of height and space. Keeping your posture erect, your shoulders back, and your head held high makes you look sure of yourself.

2. Widen your stance. When you stand with your feet close together, you can seem hesitant or unsure of what you are saying. But when you widen your stance, relax your knees and center your weight in your lower body, you look more "solid" and confident.

3. Lower your vocal pitch. In the workplace, the quality of your voice can be a deciding factor in

how you are perceived. Speakers with higher-pitched voices are judged to be less emphatic, less powerful and more nervous than speakers with lower pitched voices. One easy technique I learned from a speech therapist was to put your lips together and say "Um hum, um hum, um hum." Doing so relaxes your voice into its optimal pitch. This is especially helpful before you get on an important phone call – where the sound of your voice is so critical.

4. Try Power Priming. To display confidence and be perceived as upbeat and positive, think of a past success that fills you with pride and confidence.

5. Strike a Power Pose. Research into the effects of body posture on confidence, conducted at Harvard and Columbia Universities, has shown that simply holding your body in expansive, "high-power"

poses (leaning back with hands behind the head and feet up on a desk, or standing with legs and arms stretched wide open) for as little as two minutes stimulates higher levels of testosterone -- the hormone linked to power and dominance -- and lower levels of cortisol, a stress hormone.

6. Maintain positive eye contact. You may be an introvert, you may be shy, or your cultural background may have taught you that extended eye contact with a superior is not appropriate, but business people from the U.S., Europe, Australia (and many other parts of the world), will expect you to maintain eye contact 50-60% of the time. Here's a simple technique to improve eye contact: Whenever you greet a business colleague, look into his or her eyes long enough to notice what color they are.

7. Talk with your hands. Brain imaging has shown that a region called Broca's area, which is important for speech production, is active not only when we're talking, but also when we wave our hands. Since gesture is integrally linked to speech, gesturing as you talk can actually power up your thinking.

8. Use open gestures. Keeping your movements relaxed, using open arm gestures, and showing the palms of your hands -- the ultimate "see, I have nothing to hide" gesture -- are silent signals of credibility and candor. Individuals with open gestures are perceived more positively and are more persuasive than those with closed gestures (arms crossed, hands hidden or held close to the body, etc.) Also, if you hold your arms at waist level, and gesture within that plane, most audiences will perceive you as assured and credible.

9. Try a steeple. You see lecturers, politicians and executives use this hand gesture when they are quite certain about a point they are making. This power signal is where your hands make a "steeple" -- where the tips of your fingers touch, but the palms are separated. When you want to project conviction and sincerity about a point you're making, try steeping.

10. Reduce nervous gestures. When we're nervous or stressed, we all pacify with some form of self-touching, nonverbal behavior: We rub our hands together, bounce our feet, drum our fingers on the desk, play with our jewelry, twirl our hair, fidget -- and when we do any of these things, we immediately rob our statements of credibility. If you catch yourself indulging in any of these behaviors, take a deep breath and steady yourself by placing

your feet firmly on the floor. Stillness sends a message that you're calm and confident.

11. Smile. Smiles have a powerful effect on us. The human brain prefers happy faces, and we can spot a smile at 300 feet – the length of a football field. Smiling not only stimulates your own sense of well-being it also tells those around you that you are approachable and trustworthy.

12. Perfect your handshake. Since touch is the most powerful and primitive nonverbal cue, it's worth devoting time to cultivating a great handshake. The right handshake can give you instant credibility and the wrong one can cost you the job or the contract.

For more on Carol and her articles check;

https://www.forbes.com/sites/carolkinseygoman

"Do Not Lie to Yourself

We have to be honest about what we want and take risks rather than lie to ourselves and make excuses to stay in our comfort zone."

▯ Roy T. Bennett"

www.ingramcontent.com/pod-product-compliance
Lightning Source LLC
Chambersburg PA
CBHW071443180526
45170CB00001B/433